Married to a Suitcase

The Ultimate Solo Traveller

*Enjoy the Journey,
Olivia C Fenlon*

OLIVIA C FENLON

First published by Ultimate World Publishing 2024
Copyright © 2024 Olivia Fenlon

ISBN

Paperback: 978-1-923255-73-9
Ebook: 978-1-923255-74-6

Olivia Fenlon has asserted her rights under the Copyright, Designs and Patents Act 1988 to be identified as the author of this work. The information in this book is based on the author's experiences and opinions. The publisher specifically disclaims responsibility for any adverse consequences which may result from use of the information contained herein. Permission to use information has been sought by the author. Any breaches will be rectified in further editions of the book.

All rights reserved. No part of this publication may be reproduced, stored in or introduced into a retrieval system, or transmitted in any form, or by any means (electronic, mechanical, photocopying, recording or otherwise) without the prior written permission of the author. Any person who does any unauthorised act in relation to this publication may be liable to criminal prosecution and civil claims for damages. Enquiries should be made through the publisher.

Cover design: Ultimate World Publishing
Layout and typesetting: Ultimate World Publishing
Cover image copyrights:
sondem-Shutterstock.com
Twin Design-Shutterstock.com
Editor: Vanessa McKay

Ultimate World Publishing
Diamond Creek,
Victoria Australia 3089
www.writeabook.com.au

Testimonials

Over the past 14 years or so I have had the greatest pleasure of organising Olivia's travels and overseas adventuring. From Moldova to Mandalay, Bali to Botswana, France to Fiji and from Vietnam to Victoria Falls; Olivia always takes on each adventure with the same incredible positivity and determination in her approach. Whatever will be, will be. Olivia knows and accepts and I think relishes the fact that things occasionally happen which wouldn't be part of the plan but somehow seems to adapt to the situation. These mishaps are often the best connections and stories which come from such times. With more youthful enthusiasm than most people a third of her vintage, and a willingness to go with the flow, rolls up her sleeves and gets involved in volunteering with local charities and projects across the globe, it is no wonder that Olivia makes an impression wherever she goes. Read and take note we can all learn a lot from Olivia's travels.

Matt Chester from totally travel company.
www.totallytravel.com.au

DREAM
PERFORM
ACHIEVE
INSPIRE

I have had the pleasure of working closely with Olivia Fenlon for many years as a volunteer with the Willoughby Symphony Orchestra, Sydney Eisteddfod and other not for profit organisations.

I've been lucky to hear and read firsthand about Olivia's adventures and I feel I'm travelling with her on the same journeys as her storytelling takes you along. There are so many special paths and adventures in obscure places filled with hidden gems at the turning of every page.

I'm sure I will share many more journeys of Olivia's over the coming years but for now I hope you all share the joy I've had of being part of Olivia's stories as her friend – I consider myself very lucky to have known her for so long and discover new places through the rich tapestry of her storytelling.

Annette Brown
CEO | Sydney Eisteddfod

Mrs Annette Brown Manager of Sydney Eisteddfod P/l Sydney Australia

Dedication

I dedicate this book to my parents, Chris and George Fenlon, who were my guiding light as a child, adult, and beyond. I also thank the myriads of people I have met on my solo travels, adventures, mishaps and unbelievable encounters I never anticipated.

I thank the team of Ultimate 48 Hour Author who encouraged me to plan and complete my first Nonfiction book and I hope it won't be my last. Thank you for your support, enthusiasm, and faith that I could do it.

I wish for solo travellers to feel empowered to enjoy all the world has to offer, make new friends, and share their dreams with loved ones and fellow adventurers.

Contents

Preface and Introduction	1
Chapter One: Who am I and how did travel become my obsession?	5
Chapter Two: Wits and Wonders of solo travel - be sure of your beliefs	15
Chapter Three: 1973 and the start of my solo approach to travel	27
Chapter Four: What are people's great fears about solo travel?	37
Chapter Five: Experimenting with situations you are not familiar with	49
Chapter Six: Myths, Fibs and Reality in Solo travelling	61
Chapter Seven: Trips and adventures out of the Blue	69
Chapter Eight: Travelling Solo with Nursing in mind	81
Chapter Nine: How do I prepare to travel alone for the first time?	93
Chapter Ten: Travelling within countries in conflict	105
Annexes	121
About The Author	135

Preface and Introduction

My reasons for travelling stem mainly from curiosity about people, places and adventure.

Freedom in itinerary planning, opportunity for personal growth, and a thirst to dive headfirst into diverse cultures without distractions.

Your journey begins even before you step out of the door - with planning. Take the time to craft a well-thought-out plan. This includes setting your goals, outlining your itinerary, and ensuring you have the essentials in place.

Solo travel offers an unparalleled opportunity for personal growth. It pushes you out of your comfort zone and encourages self-reliance, adaptability, and resilience. Whether it's finding your way in new places or conquering language barriers, facing challenges head-on can greatly increase your confidence. The beauty of travelling alone is that every decision is yours alone. You choose where to go, when to leave, what sights to see (or skip), even down to where you want to eat without having to consider anyone else's preferences.

Safety should always be top priority when travelling alone; this includes choosing secure accommodations and staying informed about potential risks at your destination(s).

A key benefit often overlooked about solo travel is deeper cultural immersion. While I'm on my own in a foreign place, I'm more likely to become engaged with locals because there isn't familiar company to distract me from new experiences.

PREFACE AND INTRODUCTION

Equally important is research – diving deep into the destinations you're about to explore. Familiarise yourself with local customs, learn a few key phrases, and understand the best ways to get around.

You can tailor your travel experiences to your specific interests and passions without compromise. Whether you're into art, history, food, or adventure, you can create your ideal journey. The beauty of travelling alone is that every decision is yours alone. You choose where to go, when to leave, what sights to see (or skip), even down to where you want to eat without having to consider anyone else's preferences.

CHAPTER ONE

Who am I and how did travel become my obsession?

I am Olivia, the youngest of four siblings, and I was born with plenty of energy and an inquisitive mind. Ireland was not a very prosperous country in the mid-1940s as it had just acquired independence as a republic for 26 counties on a small island. It was also at the end of World War II in the years that I was born. My mum was a primary school teacher, and my father was a fitter and turner in the sugar factory.

We lived in a flat on the 3rd floor in the centre of the town of Carlow near Dublin. I was a curious child and was forever exploring the locality. My mum was a casual teacher. It was expected that when women married, they could no longer keep their jobs. However, my mum was rather lucky in that she was available for casual teaching positions in the absence of permanent teachers.

The requests could be short notice and there were no nursery facilities to drop off a 3-year-old for a day at short notice. Many married women remained at home and would be eager to have the opportunity to earn cash and mind a child for a few hours. My most frequent minder was Mary Parr, a single lady who lived up the street with her mum. I was a frequent bundle of fun sitting behind her in the child-chair of her bike. She knew everybody in town, and I often became the subject of conversations and was included in the conversations too, so I got used to adult chat very early in my childhood.

I would also roam around the local streets and entertain myself with other children and adults. I was fascinated by the knockers on the front doors, we didn't have one as the unit's door was inside. Women were very fond of shining the knockers and other ornamental pieces on the doors. My fascination occasionally would turn to want to tip the knocker using a bamboo stick from my father's lot in the garage. It ended when a lady noticed me as I crossed the street. She opened the door and took my stick but she got chatty with me as I explained in my childish way that I was fascinated by the glitter glow. We both made a friend that day and it became a friendship that lasted for a lifetime. I became their child, as they didn't have any. My mum was not aware of this friendship until sometime later and she was afraid that the neighbours might think she was not a good mother and was concerned about my safety. Well, it was all resolved with a visit to the Murphy's by my parents and I could go anytime I wanted.

My life became one of entertainment visiting their friends, Daddy Murphy as I called him would take me walking around the town, to shops, forges where horses were being shod, walks up the river Barrow track, and visiting houses where someone was waked after they died. I said to my mum one day that I'd been to a wake, she was expecting nightmares, asked some questions, one being did the person in the bed talk. "What… no! They were dead?"

'Aunty' Alice would take me to Dublin, the big city, or ride bikes out in the country to the Mill to collect eggs, or just to view the countryside as I got older.

They were my friends until I left school and went to Dublin to start nursing. Alice had been a psychiatric nurse before she got married. Alice died the week I left for Australia for the first time. Daddy Murphy was a frequent visitor to our house for years later.

We moved from the unit to our own home on the outer edge of the town. My father and 21 other fathers each helped each other to build their own family homes. It was a great adventure at six years to move out of the town and have a bigger area to explore and have kids my age to play sport, cricket with a bucket and hurley, or rounders, etc. Mum had become a permanent teacher at the local technical School on a yearly contract with renewal in June, so she got paid for the holidays too. But the love of her life was to return to primary school teaching, which occurred when I was 12 years. By this time, we had acquired a Morris Minor and only dad drove.

Well, move over dad as mum had to learn to drive to return to schools outside the town. The town schools were run by nuns and Christian brothers. I know where I got my tenacity from, she had a few weeks in the summer holidays to master the art of driving, but not from dad, "he wasn't a cool coach" where his car was concerned, so she got a lady from down town to coach. Mum became our coach as we arrived at driving age.

She was good, she knew all the traps, and would let you drive around the countryside for practise as they were not policed and besides you couldn't get a driver's license until you were 17 years. Our birthday present.

I had my mind made up that I was going to be a nurse at 14. Mum was concerned that the work would not be easy, but for me it would be a suitcase for travelling. I completed three certificates, paediatric, general and midwifery and now the world was mine.

I had big ideas and very little cash, but I was going to find a way to some country. The countries popular for nurses in Ireland at the time were the USA, Canada, and the Middle East. Of course, I applied and had interviews, but it was a chance accident I wrote to two hospitals in Australia, and they were begging for nurses.

I had to find a way to Melbourne that didn't cost money. Well, it happened. I rejected the ten pound holiday frequently sailing from Southampton with English families aboard, but I applied for workaway passage as a nurse and hit the target and was sailing for Melbourne in October 1970. My adventures had started, and I was a willing learner for a very exciting time in my life.

Australia brought forward many adventures, camping around Australia, working in a large hospital as operating theatre sister and I got to senior sister within two years. It would never have happened in Ireland. My adventure with local folk and fellow nurses was expanding and my promised six months soon became two years and six months. I returned to Ireland with my sister and two friends via New Zealand for three weeks, before we boarded a ship from Auckland across the Pacific through the Panama Canal to arrive back in Southampton just before Christmas, 1972.

Travelling was in my DNA and I joined up with some friends and a campervan to explore European countries and later to Scotland before returning to Ireland. Later,

WHO AM I

I left for London to work in The Middlesex Hospital in the operating theatre to complete an update program in general and neuro surgery. By October, I was bored with cold weather and not looking forward to the coming winter. I was reviewing Australia again. It didn't take long to locate a job, influence the same shipping company to repeat my workaway passage, and I was on the high seas heading to Australia.

I was an expert on the ship this time and could negotiate with crew and officers. Sailing on the high seas is an adventure in itself and every day had its own surprises. Many passengers and families travelling for the first time to Australia were met with mixed feelings. It was an advantage to have had a previous encounter with the Australian way of life and I ended up with lots of friends onboard.

I stayed with my friend near Sydney in Newcastle, and ended up working in one of the local hospitals, The Mater Hospital. I was intrigued that they would accept an outsider not trained by them, so in the interview the question of where I did my general opened the doors when I said The Mater in Dublin. The staff had mixed feelings for some time for a person who had a lot more experience, both in Australia and overseas. There were certain principles I was not prepared to change and always had my reasons if challenged.

I got interested in university education and started having a long-term romance collecting degrees both in Newcastle and eventually Sydney, which I moved to when I started my own corporate business; Update Developments Pty. Ltd. I used to convert my semester topics into seminars and facilitate them in companies as they related to Commerce and Economics useful for business. Third degree was related to Health Administration, so I could also present to medical associated organisations. I finally did Law and now I had a nice cluster which I still practise in a professional capacity in migration and sponsorship visas.

Through all the years mentioned above, I was solo travelling at every opportunity. Many around the world trips to include Ireland, European and Asian countries, which included volunteer work and Homestay situations. Solo travel has many advantages like pleasing yourself and being able to change situations at short notice. Learning from people and being able to ask for help, when needed, is important.

The advantages of Solo Travel

- Full freedom and flexibility to do whatever you want and go wherever your heart desires.
- Easier to meet new people and make new friends.
- A journey of self-discovery and personal growth, as you get to know yourself and your passions.
- Confidence boost and problem-solving skills, as you learn to be resourceful and overcome obstacles on your own.
- Time to rest and focus on the things you love.
- Spontaneity and adventure, as you can change your plans whenever you wanted to.

CHAPTER TWO

Wits and Wonders of solo travel - be sure of your beliefs

An opportunity is when you see a door opening into a whole new way of life………. Leaving familiar faces and places to volunteer in a brand-new setting can be intimidating at first. But that's the beauty of embarking on an adventure! You never know what new memories you're going to make.

When does the adventure start?

My adventures started when I investigated a nursing position in Melbourne, Australia, and was accepted almost immediately. Australia, like many countries around the world, is begging for nurses and Irish trained nurses were always welcome.

This set the ball rolling for travelling. My suitcase was already packed with three nursing certificates and it gave me the choice of what I might do on arrival in a country. I accepted the job in Melbourne and now had to get there without restrictions. Well, all requirements fell into line fairly quickly.

The job was secure at The Women's Hospital in Melbourne for two, as my sister also took the plunge.

I secured employment to do a workaway passage as a nurse on the Castle Felice, one of Sitmar's Italian Fleet line transporting migrant families to Australia on what was described as the £10 holiday. People paid £10 to secure a passage to Australia and signed up to remain in Australia for two years to repay the Government for the 'gift'. I was not included in this arrangement as I was an independent passenger and arriving in Australia with a job prospect on arrival.

I had a short holiday in London visiting all the historic areas and enjoying the entertainment on stage with Tito Gobi in Fiddler on the roof.

The Castle Felice was our next home for six weeks + anchored in Southampton

We took off for the ship in Southampton called the Castle Felice and my first overseas job waiting for me in Melbourne and six weeks of experience nursing on board a sea liner. I felt all my Christmases had come at once.

Meeting up with our ship at Southampton, meeting the crew, and finding out our allocations to working on board was exciting.

When opportunity knocks are you ready to grab it and make it happen?

I was to have many more opportunities come unannounced in my life, but are you ready to grab them and make the most out of the situation to your advantage?

Life on the ocean was a far cry from traditional nursing in Ireland, and I was so excited that my constant reply when asked if I was married was, "Oh yes, I am married to a suitcase."

What a life aboard a cruise ship it was, one long holiday of clinical nursing, socialising, getting to know about migrants to Australia and their high hopes of a better life in what was advertised as a sunny country. Along the way, we stopped at the Canary Islands, Cape Town in South Africa and the Capetown Rollers in the high seas. Our first stop in Australia was Fremantle, then Perth, and finally Melbourne.

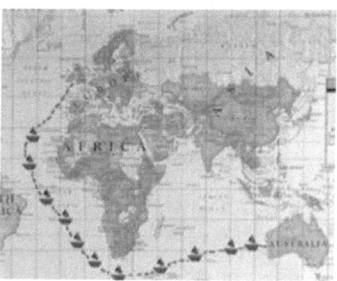

We arrived in Melbourne and dropped anchor in what was a glorious sunny morning and were whisked away by a representative from the Women's Hospital, which we had settled for. As it was a weekend, we met our longtime friend Pat and family, and stayed for the weekend and got to our meeting With the Director of Nursing on Monday. I took up my position in the operating theatre after a discussion about conditions, and my sister took the maternity wards.

My dreams had born fruit, and I was really looking forward to our adventure in Melbourne, for six months anyway. Well, it stretched into two and a half years, of exciting travel in a country as big as the USA but with long distances between cities. Within two years, I transitioned from being a newcomer 'sister' to a senior sister in the department, which would never have occurred in Ireland.

There were many opportunities on offer in this big country, both in the professional field and in the tourist travel spots.

Our travels took us to Canberra, a city of circles that was like a maze to get out of. Tasmania was our first camping event and full of surprises, getting meals and erecting tents. The scenery is spectacular in Tassie as it is lovingly called, especially the inland with Cradle Mountain National Park, mountains and snow patches which Australians found exciting, snow and cold weather were not my speciality and was to become a deciding factor in travel and choosing places for jobs in the future. You learn a lot about yourself when you travel.

Our longest and most exciting trip was to do a 51-day camping trip around the full perimeter of the coast of Australia, with a dip into the centre – Alice Springs and Uluru, then called Ayres Rock after the supposed English explorer, who found it long after the Aboriginals, had been using it as their citadel for centuries.

What a trip! It was packed with variety, from the east coast and its spectacular beaches, towns and vegetation to dry dusty interiors and thousands of kms of land and no habitat from the northern territory except for Darwin and Kakadu national park, until you reached Alice Springs and Uluru.

The trip included all the major cities from Sydney to Brisbane to Darwin, Alice Springs, down the west coast of Australia to Perth and across the Nullarbor to Adelaide and Melbourne return. What a trip never to be forgotten.

Some of the learning points that live with me:

You get the feel for the size of Australia and how much time is spent getting from A to B. The cost of travel is often higher than overseas trips to the nearby Asian ports and were quite a draw card for many Australians for cheap holidays.

Australian conversation is full of slang words never heard of before and often left you puzzled with mixed feelings about what really was discussed. This led to many funny outcomes and awkward moments as you worked out what was expected and what was not expected. You need to laugh at yourself and not take yourself too seriously.

By the time we had arrived in Darwin in the Northern Territory, it was the wet season. We had been warned about its unpredictability by our friends in Melbourne who had introduced this tour to us, they had completed it the previous year and warned us to, "Make sure you put your backpack and clothes on a camp stool overnight, as you may get an unexpected downpour overnight." And it certainly happened to us on our last night in Darwin and we were one of the few people who had dry clothes for the following day.

Northern Territory travel was mostly dry and very isolated from daily living and easy access to shops, so you had to use a lot of imagination for both camping, keeping food fresh, and also carrying water. We had some fun. My sister went to get some water from the container in the coach and when I put it on the cereal the next morning, I realised it was petrol so we had to get rid of that.

Camping is exciting and certainly highly unpredictable. We did most of our showers in any little pool that presented itself at morning break or at lunchtime and there were plenty in the Northern Territory, such as Geike Gorge, Halls Gap, and the Carr Boyd Ranges with surprised waterfalls.

Getting onto the west coast of Australia was such a relief as we were close to the coast and had many stops and dips to keep cool and calm. We were now into our 30th day of the trip.

On our way back to Melbourne, we passed many Aboriginal sites like Wave Rock, which is adorned with aboriginal carvings and it's a beautifully layered colour of the different rock formations. Kalgoorlie is the mining area and has a very rich outputs of coal and minerals, that certainly puts Western Australia on the economic map.

The Nullarbor Desert stretches from Perth to Adelaide and we were glad to get close to Adelaide because by then we had not seen showers for nearly three days and everybody rushed to have a decent shower before dinner. We camped in Port Augusta for our last night camping and the following day we took the last leg of our trip back to Melbourne, after 51 days.

Back to work we went, motivated by our desire to earn money for travel and to discover the captivating surroundings, both inland and by the ocean. Our favourite destination is Phillip Island, where we camped near the beach and witness the amazing sight of small noisy penguins returning to shore to feed their young. It's so loud that it's almost deafening. Of course, today it's now very commercialised and is not anything like what we enjoyed so much in the early 70s.

Change often comes in the most unexpected places.

I never thought I would leave Australia. I had so much planned to see and do, but life changed when I saw an advertisement for positions in London for people who were interested in furthering their experience in operating theatres. It appealed to me because it was very much a practical program rather than a theory program which would work for me. I applied and quickly got accepted and commenced the program towards the end of 1973. I found this an exciting adventure and also it would provide added experience in the general area and modern operation techniques in the cardiac and brain sections.

We returned to Ireland at the end of 1972 in the company of our two greatest friends, Valerie and Charlotta, who were also returning to England to complete their maternity qualifications on leave from the hospital. So, life goes on and all the cards fall into place as if it's meant to happen, which is really my mantra for the rest of my life.

Planning to leave Australia 1972

I delayed the start of the program until September 1973, as my friend Judy was coming over to Ireland and England in the summer of '73 and we were planning our next trip to take place in Europe while she was here.

Our time in Melbourne finished in 1972 and I appreciated my time and experience gained at The Women's Hospital, both practical and personal recognition of my previous education and experience, which I shared with my colleagues.

Learning points

1. Are you ready for an opportunity when it presents itself?
2. What are the advantages and disadvantages of the position?
3. What do you hope to get from the situation?
4. What do you need in writing before starting the job?
5. Is it time for me to go solo in the future? A definite "YES"

CHAPTER THREE

1973 and the start of my solo approach to travel

Travelling solo is not for the faint-hearted, as fear of the unknown can be a strong deterrent and the 'What ifs' are often exaggerated before one even ventures out to travel.

1973 was a fantastic year, and it was also the year I decided I would travel solo or at least make my own arrangements. I started working in Dublin doing agency nursing work and I always knew that nursing would be my ticket to solo travelling. I had many private cases and was involved with the new territory of kidney transplants and very excited to be part of that process. Never short of work or money, there was always a call to work if you needed it.

I always called nursing my suitcase to pickup and take-off to any job in nursing. Later in life, when travelling in Asia and teaching English as a second language (ESL) the kids would ask "Are you married?" I would say, "Yes, I am married to a suitcase." This always drew some laughs when they got the meaning. I carried that suitcase around Ireland with jobs in Dublin, Carlow and Kilkenny and agency work specialising in new areas of medicine such as transplants.

Some of the great fears of travelling solo of course are:

- Worrying about being lonely.
- Not liked by people in selected jobs.
- Concerns about safety.
- Mobility issues could be a challenge.
- The most important one, of course, is culture shock.
- Fear of not liking the food in another country.

Our European trip in a campervan 1973.

I organised a trip to include my friend Judy from Australia, my friend in Ireland and older sister. What a way to enjoy the 4th of July, Independence Day for the USA.

We were ready for our trip in Europe, which started in Ostend and took us through many countries such as:

Luxembourg - a tiny state squeezed in between France, Belgium and Germany, we thought we would just pass through. Soon delayed us in exploring its castles, churches, walking trips with guides, vineyards and leafy streets. Free city transport since 2020 is a great asset.

Bavaria - is one of Germany's most widely known and scenic travel destinations. Neuschwanstein, the most well-known castle, and one of many in the Bavarian Alps and looks straight out of a fairy tale. Take the cable car to get the best views, plenty of Alpine lakes for Kayaking or relaxing and to swoon over, and of course the great Oktoberfest to witness the true Bavarian spirit.

Austria - is so well known after the *Sound of Music* you can't leave without taking your own photos in and on the memorable locations. **Salzburg** is a wonderful city both in daytime and night life, especially around the Christmas markets. Traditional singing and drinking offer both entertainment and cultural immersion.

Italy - took in the northern top and included **Lake Como** and the Alps so spectacular and never to be forgotten. **Venice** and the great tourist attractions,

1973 AND THE START OF MY SOLO APPROACH

gondolas, churches, bridges and customs. A week can slip by without notice.

France at Menton - on the Mediterranean coast. What great memories came back, as I did my first volunteer work with a family in a small village perched on the side of the mountains overlooking the Cote-de-Azure **Saint Agnes.** Well worth a visit. Have breakfast there overlooking the Italian riviera. And also, dinner at night as the coastal lights flicker.

Grenoble - and the French Alps is a must if you are driving, Grenoble Alpes is a land of hiking, skiing, canyoning and MTB. It is also a land of excellence and a favourite for champions, who have Olympics in mind both summer and winter sports. The old scene of the Olympics in Grenoble begs to have your photos taken as a champion.

The scenery is magnetic as it changes at every turn.

Finally, back to **Ostend** and into **London.**

Scotland and Northern England

I took my mum to the towns and cities in Scotland that had a traditional background. I don't need a guide when my mum is the guide and has all the facts and funny stories to go with the delivery. Her diary takes the form of poetry of which I take out to recap both her Australian trip and this one.

Scotland's highlights, from its capital city to mountains and beautiful islands,

Chester is a unique Roman city and is a wonder to visit, surrounded by Roman walls, cobbled streets, markets, and its post, can take up days of your time. Some great battles come to mind about the War of the Roses and changes of kingship. Many old Roman ruins are discovered regularly and are very well preserved and displayed.

Hadrian's Wall that separated Scotland from England is a great attraction to walkers.

Skye was on our agenda but the weather was not co-operating, so we took part in Scottish Highland games on the west coast before we crossed over to the East coast through the mountains and Lakes to Dunfermline the home of the famous USA philanthropist, Andrew Carnegie.

Aberdeen on the East Coast is another great city to explore, situated on the Dee River. It overlooks the offshore petroleum industry. There are gardens to relax in and country walks to stretch your legs.

Edinburgh the capital, has so much history you could spend a lifetime and feel you have only scratched the surface. The Edinburgh Festival and Tattoo have world-wide recognition. Its new parliament building is worth a visit, it is very modern. Many of the buildings around the city are an architect's paradise.

We returned to London by the M1 and dropped off the campervan with much reluctance, as it had been our home for weeks. All good things end, but the memories live on for a lifetime.

London became my home for a year to complete a program at the Middlesex Hospital in the heart of London. I was quick to immerse myself not only in the program but also in the extraordinary and magnetic city of London and all it has to offer.

I used to visit Covent Garden and Coliseum often, buying pre-tickets for performances and sitting in the inexpensive God's section.

I was a frequent visitor to places like **Hampton Court, Tower of London, Westminster** Abbey, Stonehenge by bus, Edinburgh and Aberdeen for a cousin's wedding, and just missed the Edinburgh Tattoo.

Frequent solo dinners out where I love to observe people in restaurants. It is one of the most frequent worries of solo travellers feeling awkward or conspicuous being on their own. Of course, it can attract other loners to your table, but you have the right to smile sweetly and decline. Looking preoccupied with a book or phone often prevents the intrusion.

When Opportunity knocks, are you ready to take on the adventure?

I returned to Australia before winter set in and I was lucky the second time around to get a working passage from Sitmar on the Fairstar and Australia's house gift of permanent residence to return was my biggest surprise. Visas were introduced in 1975 and my previous time in Australia counted towards getting the visa.

The benefits of Solo Travel

<u>You are your own boss, and you can make or break the rules without discussions</u>

It prevents the following:
- Wasting time getting everyone in a group to agree.
- Relationship woes from differing opinions.
- General tension.

CHAPTER FOUR

What are people's great fears about solo travel?

There are two types of procrastinators: passive and active procrastinators.

1. Passive procrastinators: delay the task because they have trouble making decisions and acting on them. Sometimes they are perfectionists and making an ad hoc decision is not their practise. Unfortunately, the opportunity may not last or ever return.

2. Active procrastinators: delay the task purposefully because working under pressure allows them to

"feel challenged and motivated", or they can blame someone if the results are not to their liking.

I was in awe of the full ship of migrants when I took the cruise from Southampton to Melbourne as a workaway nurse. It was made up of parents and children travelling to the far end of the world must have been the most daunting experience of a lifetime for the parents. I was pumped up about my doing exactly the same thing as they were doing. I grabbed the opportunity as it met my needs to get to Australia cash free and take on the nursing job I was offered without interview.

If decisions didn't turn out well or lack of having planned properly, I can't blame the world. I leave out the 'What-ifs' until they happen, a lesson learned from my mother. She used to say, "Wait until the bridge presents itself, then take action." Best advice ever.

What to do with some fears raised:

Travelling alone

Doubts and fears are there to keep us safe. But they can also be unnecessarily paralysing. It's this side of travel fear that I'd like to address.

WHAT ARE PEOPLE'S GREAT FEARS

One of the first steps in facing any fear is to name it. Break it down to see the source of the fear and determine whether it makes sense. Below is a list of reasons people might be afraid of travelling alone.

Worry about being lonely: there are times when you will miss your family, your friends, cafes you like to visit, pictures you'd like to go to, yes you will miss home.

Adopt a more positive view

- Read up about the places you're going to and what you might like to see.
- The locals will know you are foreign and may want to practise their English with you.
- Friendship is a two-way process. Just smiling and saying hello is a good start.
- How people live, and work varies around the world, but that's the attraction in travelling.
- They also come from a family and are eager to share and welcome you into their country, so enjoy the journey and seize the opportunities.

Concern about one's own safety:

- One can't forecast the future so living in the present is easier to make a decision and leave out the 'what ifs'. If a situation arises, then make your plan to move out of the danger.

Some tips to remain safe when travelling alone.

- Control the itinerary and choose the activities that suit your interests and preferences.
- Try new food and immerse yourself in local culture by reading articles associated with your places.
- Pack lighter and carry good identification in more than one place.
- Meet new people and interact with them. A great way is to learn their language. Get an interpretation App on your mobile phone or carry a separate multi-language translator devise lets you translate any language instantly without any internet connection.
- Learn more about yourself and work up the courage to take calculated risks.
- Focus on your surroundings and trust your intuition.

Many people feel awkward when eating alone and there are multiple reasons for this. Again, try to work out the reason why so you can solve something definite.

WHAT ARE PEOPLE'S GREAT FEARS

Some reasons being:

- People looking at you may not necessarily mean they are.
- Try reading a book or menu.
- If they ask to sit with you say NO with a smile on your face.
- I learn from studying people in the cafes, body Language etc., what works and doesn't work.

Health challenges and pre-existing conditions:

- Be medically fit to travel.
- Buy insurance coverage at the time of your first trip deposit or shortly thereafter (time frame varies by company). You may only be paying a deposit, but should any major disaster strike, you will be covered by your insurance.
- Ensure that any pre-existing condition is stable.
- Insure full cost of trip and your insurance cover for emergency evacuation. Flights are expensive and getting emergency booking may not be covered.

Mobility issues are a challenge:

Dealing with physical limitations in travel. Restricted mobility is a common concern as people age. Furthermore, people can have congenital disabilities from birth, and age does not differentiate in terms of susceptibility.

Some points to consider:

- Identifying your disabilities and can they be covered by insurance and the trip you plan.
- Clear with your doctor or medical people associated with your treatment, may give you checklists.
- Bring sufficient medications for your trip and prescription orders for additional doses.
- Find out if you need to bring equipment with you, or can you get it where you are going.

Cruises are becoming very popular for all ages. The ship is equipped with elevators to accommodate individuals with disabilities and must adhere to jurisdictional requirements. Moreover, shore excursions are not mandatory, giving travellers the freedom to select what suits them.

- Look for destinations with modern facilities, mostly in new construction and high rises since elevators would be required making it easier to use wheelchairs and scooters. Do your homework in advance, chat with groups online to check what's available and what might be of use for your trip.
- Find out if you can rent scooters or other aids at your destination for short periods. If you cannot, check requirements for meeting enhanced security for travel through airports and ships.

Culture shock is a very common problem with people travelling even in a group, but especially on their own. No matter how much you read up about the location that is foreign to you will never really feel the impact of it until you land new in the middle of it.

- Learn about your destination, the customs, mode of dress, manners, the food. You may not agree with them, but you are in their country.
- Try eating out in cafes, in your own country and see what you like and don't like.

- Culinary travel tips for food and wine travel planning. Avoid lukewarm food or reheated food. When serving from a buffet or salad bar, make sure the hot food is steaming and the cold food is chilled. Germs that cause food poisoning grow quickly in hot climates.
- Make sure the packets are sealed completely and dry. Use safe water, boiled water, to make up formula for babies. Wash fruit before eating, especially if bought at markets. Tap water in foreign countries is not always safe. Carry water purifier tablets, easy to carry and use if you are not sure. Drop 1-2 in a bottle of water depending on the size, leave overnight in the fridge and you are ready to travel the next day. And you can prepare a refill while you are out and about.

Studying abroad: Students living alone in a foreign country face significant culture shock. Without parental support, they can feel more anxious about adjusting to a new culture, especially when the patterns of communication are significantly different. If not handled properly before the trip, this can have long-lasting effects on students, so universities and families need to provide well-rounded programs to help them face these challenges. Psychology reports are worth reading in these areas as student exchange programs are very popular and on the increase.

Struggling with a new climate: An under-examined feature of homesickness is dealing with the weather. For example, many Australians in Canada complain about the long, cold winters, and end up returning to the warm beaches of Australia because they just can't handle the cold. I notice when I returned to Ireland in their summer, it's not even as hot as our spring. I always seem to wear winter clothing or certainly clothing borrowed from my own sisters, as I don't want to have to carry them in my baggage.

High humidity can be a problem for people that are not used to it, and they certainly need to take care with regard to their hydration as they lose a lot of fluid through perspiration. The list of differences is vast and can only be experienced when you actually make the move to a different country. It is good practice to make sure you read about the climate changes within the country that you're likely to be visiting especially those who are volunteering or on exchange programs.

MARRIED TO A SUITCASE

Avoid reading and watching the media if they make you anxious, especially prior to volunteering your time in a foreign country, air travelling, or extended long trips overseas. The media does not show all the good happenings around the world, just the bad. They are dramatic and extreme. If the news makes you anxious, stop watching it before you travel. Go cold turkey on the crime shows as well. Read more about safe travelling and exciting outcomes that the average person has enjoyed and wants you to know so you will be attracted.

Plan to be safe. There's a difference between worrying unnecessarily about the world not being safe and planning to be safe, just as you have to do at home. No place is truly safe. We still have to take care even in our own country. We get sudden events that are horrific. As I write today, there was a fatal holdup in Bondi Shopping centre and many people lost their lives just doing normal activities. Become familiar with areas that are safe versus areas that are considered to be unsafe, unless you want extreme outcomes.

Some techniques that can help in planning your trip and enjoying the experience.

1. Learn successful money-saving techniques.
2. Develop travel planning skills for a trip you'll love.
3. Understand your travel strengths and abilities even if you haven't travelled before.
4. Discover which travel resources deliver more travel for less money.
5. Fine-tune your senses to enjoy the wonder in this world.
6. Plan for a safe and exciting trip.

Concern for pets

Concern for pets is common when away from them for short or long periods. Making sure you have a trustworthy person to agree to take care and let them know what would help you and them while you are away. Some people like to have photo update of their pets and sharing on Whatsapp.com or similar sources.

CHAPTER FIVE

Experimenting with situations you are not familiar with

Solo travel teaches us about the relationship between solitude and loneliness, how to deal with both the ups and downs of being alone, what's most important in life, and lets us improve in so many ways; personal growth is the name of the game. All that is left is for you to get out there and experience it for yourself. www.goabroad.com

How to Plan to Travel Alone

If you have decided that you have the confidence, that you are comfortable in your own company, and that you can take care of your safety, you may have decided that you will travel solo independently. You may not always be alone, you can mix your holiday or break with a group trip, and socialising with the people around you and families if you are involved with ESL (English second language), either improving your own English or somebody else's.

Here are some suggestions:

Know what is required legally for the country or countries you plan to visit. Crossing borders can be tricky especially in Africa and some Asian countries. Visas vary between single entry to multi-entry. Single entry only allows one entry to the country. If you accidently cross the border with a single-entry visa, you will not be able to return. This can happen easily if you are near borders and may be doing volunteer work. The family members may not be aware of the difference between visas, and they are helpless to help you if it occurs. You will have to go to the nearest embassy and get a visa that will allow access.

Before you leave, be sure you understand the visa requirements and spend a few moments to understand the currency exchange. Make sure your passport doesn't expire for at least three months after your departure date. Some ask for six months after your trip ends, know the countries expectations before you go. Most travel agents will draw your attention to requirements necessary, make sure you read and understand the content. Booking online without a travel agent can leave you open to a number of traps.

Make a budget.

Know how you are going to travel in advance and pay up front for flights and trains before you leave if possible. Investigate if there are Travel Passes for visitors, especially places like Japan where you order the voucher in advance before your arrival and change it at the airport on arrival for a travel ticket to use on public transport. You will have to pay if you travel on private buses or trains. Most transport in Kyoto is private so your travel ticket won't cover you.

Also make sure that your flights arrive at a reasonable hour. Daylight is preferable to arrive at any port but especially if it's a new place. Travelling by trains late at night in a strange country is stressful, make friends with passengers if they are getting off at the same station. Japanese people are very helpful and can guide the taxi drivers to where you need to go.

Book your accommodation. Like flights, it is good to book in advance and pre-paying reduces the stress. Some hotels run shuttle services to the airport. Some Bali hotels near the new airport have free hourly shuttles that pick you up and also return you to the airport.

Mobile phones with an app to locate places are useful, sim cards can be online or physical card. Keep the phone numbers on your phone so they are accessible when you land.

There is a big push to have carry-on baggage, so check the weights. They may vary from country to country, airline to airline. Some airlines are very strict about weight and what you can carry for free and then you pay excess which can be a shock. This usually happens on your return journey when you are carrying gifts back to family, etc.

Arrive at the airport, train, or bus station early. Whether it's traffic congestion or a massive lineup at the airport, many things can slow you down when trying to catch a flight. If your hotel or residence is not near the airport you might consider booking into a hotel near the airport for an overnight stay. Less stressful than trying to get through congested traffic at rush hours, especially in the large Asian cities.

Plan little for your first day. Take the time to settle in and get to know the city and how it works. Do people line up for the bus? What's the street food like and where are the busiest stands? What's within walking distance of your lodging? Take it slow and learn. Most hotels carry information about the city transport and taxi, etc. Usually, you can get free maps of the streets and places of interest.

If you are planning to travel outside your own environment, I can guarantee you would have challenges and unfamiliar situations to deal with. Personally, I think that's all part of the enjoyment of the holiday. Some people adapt easier than others, and it's important to find positive coping mechanisms to get you through the changes. Adjusting to situations that are constantly changing will take some effort and some time. Personally, I see this as part of the excitement of my holidays over many decades, that is meeting new people in new situations and adjusting to the level of acceptance by them. Often hotels can arrange a 'buddy' at a cost to explore the city or places of interest.

Your experience, both past and present, will help you shape how you adapt to unfamiliar situations. If you're having trouble working through change, counselling services can help you talk through the motions. If this is your first time and you have little experience operating on your own may be good for you to have people you can talk to, could be a friend, could be a counsellor, people from the country, consulates who may have information and would like to talk to you about it. It does depend on where you want to go and what you want to see.

Some hints to think about:

How well you adapt to changes, different people and expectations, how observant you are.

Being open-minded means being receptive to new ideas, information, and arguments which I like to call a difference of opinion. Everybody is different and can be even more different when you meet them in compromising situations.

My advice is to read up as much as you can about the areas that you are planning to go to, especially where volunteer jobs are concerned. Can I bring some of my experience from home with me? How you do you shop, cross a street, etc.

EXPERIMENTING WITH SITUATIONS

Believe in yourself, identify times when to get yourself free from a problem. I call mistakes experiences I can learn from.

Don't panic at the unexpected. Take time to review the situation and check how you can move forward, where to get help. Basic problem solving is required.

You are number one when travelling. If you join a group there is a risk that they may not have the same ideas or expectations for selected activities, so check what's expected and decide if you want to participate.

If disagreements arise in a group, ask open ended questions … Who? Where? What? Why? And how? Gather information and see who agrees or disagrees. Use primary words to move forward, I would like to do…. or not participate in an event. Many trips included extreme sport or activities, like skateboarding, bungee jumping, snowboarding, mountain climbing, and are a big attraction to young adults. Make sure your insurance covers you for these situations, both for treatment, transport and evacuation home if ongoing treatment is required. The average travel insurance may not have evacuation available and you can get stranded until you can pay the medical bill.

If I'm travelling around cities, I always carry identification with me, which is usually a laminated photocopy of my passport and an emergency number at the back. I also carry a handwritten card of maybe a place that I want to go to, and I will often ask in the hotel or the hostel or the group I am staying with if you could write it in the language of the country. I certainly have got to my destination sometimes longer than I had anticipated but I've got there all the same.

If you are confronted with a situation that you are challenged by, be honest, don't make up stories or exaggerate the situation. See how the other party feels about the situation and see how you may be able to come to an agreement without blaming others and staying positive.

Solo travel boosts your self-confidence to operate on your own

One thing your friends and family will recognise immediately when you return home is your newfound sense of confidence. You would be better personally after: for example - getting lost, experimenting with new hobbies, meeting new people, pushing yourself to your limits, and experiencing how much you can take.

You will know how to operate well under pressure, be a better decision-maker, a better communicator, and know yourself better than ever. You will have earned a new understanding of life, and it will be evident, so make the most of it and carry it through to your life at home.

Summary

How to be comfortable in a new situation which is really a summary of what we have discussed above as a shortlist:

- Be yourself.
- Monitor your own body language.
- Ask questions from other people.
- Keep your boundaries in mind - they may need to be discussed.
- Be intentional on getting an agreement.
- Prepare in advance if you know there's going to be meeting.
- Start small, keep your words primary, and stay on the point to get a result.
- Clarity on the plan forward.
- Avoid cliché People often dismiss your concerns as silly and not important by using replies without knowing the reason behind the concern. Replies like: No problem! Happy to help but! Of course….! Nothing to worry about….! These do not solve your problem.

- Thank people for their helpful information.
- If there is a problem, find out what it is first before discussing the outcome. Stay on track and share the outcome.
- Say "NO" without being rude. I'd love to but… reason. I'm busy, I can't, my apology…

CHAPTER SIX

Myths, Fibs and Reality in Solo travelling

Everyone who travels has a tale to tell. Sometimes the information is partly true and partly fiction in what they would have liked their holiday to be. So sometimes you have to separate the fact from the fiction in order to uncover the truth behind their stories. In most cases with regard to travelling you have to separate the facts from what really happened and what you expected to happen and never did. Travelling solo provides many situations that will educate you about how to negotiate your way through holidays in general, also about people you meet on holidays and especially volunteer jobs. No amount of reading and research will fully equip you for what lies ahead, just wait and see what happens and then apply your skills and questions to learn more.

Let's dive into some common travel myths and fibs and exaggerations to uncover the truth behind them.

MYTH 1: TRAVEL IS VERY EXPENSIVE.

It depends on what you want from travel and your personal expectations. Volunteer work which varies in costs depends on the type you choose. **Homestay**, very common in America/Canada/ and across Europe and Asia, may acknowledge the hours worked in leu of lodging and rent. In Asia you need to be careful about using board and lodging in exchange for teaching over an extended period, usually a month or more, may attract attention if your visa is purely for a tourist. Fines can be quite high if caught. Entry to do volunteer work is usually a tourist visa and specifically says, not for employment. A volunteer enters the country as a visitor and visas have a specific length.

REALITY: While there are certainly luxurious and pricey ways to travel, it's entirely possible to see the world on a budget. Holidays range from super luxurious to budgeting for the same area without the high cost. To enjoy trips, you need to have an interest in where you go and how to get there. Travel is only a means to an end. It takes you to where you have planned to interact with the locals and enjoy the beauty it has to offer.

Work-away passage can be a means to an end on ships, if you have the right skills and qualifications for the job. A common skill/s is nursing as it can be used in almost all areas that include people.

Nothing ventured nothing gained ....so advertise yourself and your talents and you may be surprised with the input it will deliver.

MYTH 2: THE BEST DEALS ARE ALWAYS FOUND AT THE LAST MINUTE

REALITY: Last minute deals can be a surprise package but don't always live up to the advertisement. Most holiday destinations that are popular around the world are booked well in advance and rarely provide what they advertise or sometimes our expectations for a budget price are way above what's advertised, which leads to disappointments.

Have a good travel agent who is well versed in your needs, requirements, and is used to booking your trips with your preferences - such as volunteer work to be included in trips.

I work within a budget and I always get more satisfaction from my volunteer work than the commercial trips, as they allow me to see locations without losing my need to explore alone. I use Intrepid, an Australian company that provides a variety of big adventures both in Australia and overseas. The trips are affordable at a base price and offers additional trips of choice at the traveller's expense and include extreme sports, walking trips, winter sports, etc. check out the company at www.intrepidtravel.com

MYTH 3: YOU'LL GET THE BEST PHOTOS AT ICONIC LANDMARKS

While iconic sites are popular for a reason, sometimes the most memorable and unique photos come from off-the-beaten-path locations or candid moments. At the very least, snapping memorable holiday moments in volunteer jobs especially as they are personal and each student has a name.

I have some wonderful shots taken to have and to hold for a lifetime. Google running my photos at random on the computer to jog my memory especially as I get older keeps my mind active having to recall the location and the people involved.

MYTH 4: YOU NEED TO BE FLUENT IN THE LOCAL LANGUAGE

REALITY: Most tourist destinations have signs expressed in English and many locals often understand simple English, so communicating basic needs isn't a major challenge. Knowing the local language is a plus and the locals certainly appreciate it, even if they do find your pronunciation amusing. Translation apps and phrase books can help bridge any communication gaps, so there's no need to learn another language before you travel, although a few key phrases can be fun.

A good tip in a strange place to locate a place or station in the city is to write it down and may get one of the locals to indicate how to get there in both English and the local language. Sometimes they will escort you and an opportunity for them to practice speaking English. You may even get an invitation to meet their family, have a cup of coffee, or a chat.

MYTH 5: IT'S NOT SAFE TO TRAVEL solo

REALITY: Solo travel today is widely practised. It depends mainly on your destination and how you prepare for it. Many places are solo-traveller-friendly and have infrastructures to support them. The principles apply to groups as well as solo ramblers to monitoring your belongings in crowded places and drinking responsibly will go a long way to ensuring your personal safety, whether at home or abroad. As always, research is crucial. Many solo travellers join communities online who can provide invaluable advice and support.

Some of these requirements are never printed in a book. They vary from one country to another and you are likely to find out when something actually happens to you. It is good practise to investigate what countries you are going to visit and what requirements you will need if you are targeted.

MYTH 6: HOSTELS ARE ONLY FOR YOUNG BACKPACKERS

REALITY: Hostels and accommodation are available with single rooms but no meals provided, but nearly all of them had a bathroom or one between two which you often find in volunteer jobs. Volunteering often involves dormitory-style accommodation, but you can opt for a single supplement for a small fee, which typically includes a private room with a personal shower and toilet.

Loud parties carried on late at night and items that mysteriously go missing will be investigated in any of the volunteer hostels or premises. Japan, Tokyo advertise single room with a retama style bedding, that you could roll up during the day, makes the room look bigger and comfortable. Being close to railway station is a bonus as you can find your landmarks to return home. It had a kitchen you could cook meals or chat to other travellers and close to shops where you could get a vast variety of takeaways, quite easily and very cheaply.

MYTH 7: YOU MUST VISIT EVERY TOP ATTRACTION

REALITY: Travel is a personal journey. It's okay to skip the 'must-see' sites in favour of what genuinely interests you. Sometimes, the best memories are made wandering through local neighbourhoods or stumbling upon unexpected gems. Allowing yourself time to soak in the atmosphere around you can often provide a more authentic and wholistic experience of the destination than any crowded and noisy tourist trap can ever offer.

MYTH 8: DUTY-FREE MEANS THE CHEAPEST SHOPPING

Duty-free is always a big attraction to visitors but in fact what you usually get in the airport is as high as or higher than if you were paying tax. So, it is fun to bargain with the shops and markets. Get into the practice of checking out the local stores and markets for items that you would like and are often at a much lower price as an attraction for you to buy from the locals rather than the airport.

It does give you an opportunity to test your bargaining skills. Asian countries and some European cities have markets and the owners like bargaining, it's fun. A great excuse to go shopping and get some bargains but also to enjoy their company and get to know more about their city or country. Use translators if you don't know the language, it helps to ask questions.

The locals are very good at bargaining and expect you to offer some reasonable prices which you are more likely to get if the offers are not insulting.

CHAPTER SEVEN

Trips and adventures out of the Blue

Trips and plans have developed from small requests and lead to bigger and better trips than ever imagined. Most of the trips following started with a small request not associated with the outcome, but it left a legacy never to be forgotten.

Peru, the top of the pops for a fantastic trip No. 1

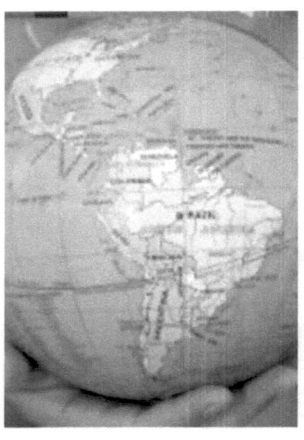

Peru started with a simple request to help a friend to improve her English. We had an exchange, I teach and she shared lunch, she was a great cook.

She was going back to Peru for a visit and the flight was discounted. Would I come too, WOW what an invitation. My travel agent Matt and I came up with a fantastic holiday and included:

- Volunteer job on an archaeological site in Lima.
- Visit to Cuzco for a week to get used to altitude
- Complete a five-day hike to Machu Picchu
- Lake Titicaca, Colca Canyon, Arequipa, Inca trail, rainbow mountain.

Some good suggestions if interested in this trip,

- Archaeological sites are usually open to the weather and hot sun, so take the usual

- precautions to prevent sun burn, dehydration, accidents, etc.
- If doing Machu Picchu I suggest to spend a few days in Cusco to climatise to the altitude, before your trek. It's not a walk in the park, spectacular as it is, and you walk for five days. Most people never make it because their body systems have not adjusted to the high altitudes and its effects on one's body.
- The hike is strenuous but the sherpas make it bearable with their wonderful cooking and also carrying our 6 Kilo allowance pack and setting up our camp and tents for the night.
- It's so worth making the trip just to stand at the top of the Monkey Steps and the view the scene from the Sun Gate and know you made it.
- We all slept on the train back to Cusco for a sleep in a proper bed.

Fantastic trip No. 2 Was making my way to Australian for the first time.

<u>Nothing Ventured, Nothing Gained</u>

Getting my first workaway passage in 1970 came as a result of a very short handwritten letter to a number of shipping companies that sailed between UK and Australia.

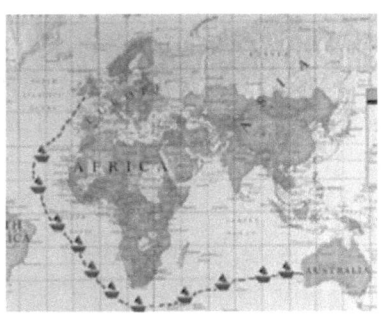

24th of February 1970

Dear Sir

I would like to enquire, if it is at all possible to work one's passage to Australia on board one of your liners, in whatever capacity you think suitable. My sister and I are both registered general nurses and sick children's nurses also midwifery. We have arranged for nursing positions in a hospital in Melbourne 4 August 1970, but due to delay in the assisted passage scheme, we will be unable to accept the positions. We could travel any time after May 1970. Hoping to hear from you at your earliest convenience.

Thanking you in advance
yours sincerely
Olivia C Fenlon

- This drew a response from two companies well known at the time, Sitmar and the other Chandris. This led to one of the greatest adventures of my life, as it took us from one end of the world to the other which only cost me time and labour rather than cash output.
- Sitmar also came to the rescue, when I decided after my return to Ireland and later wanted to return to Australia in 1974, provided a work-away passage all because of a report that was written about me in 1970.
- We had quite a laugh about it at the time, but I was certainly deeply indebted to Sitmar for its generosity.
- I am a firm believer in taking a chance no matter how simple it looks. If it's meant to motivate somebody to action, then you have achieved your goal.

Fantastic trip No. 3 – My Trip to Africa never to be forgotten

This is a trip of a lifetime to a lot of people

Africa is like no other trips that I have done, as it does not compare with other countries, it is just so unique and extraordinary.

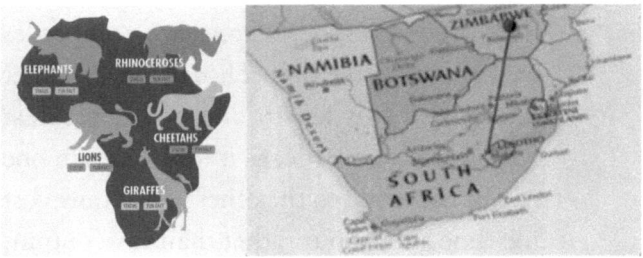

What do you need to get to Africa?

- Prior to this trip you need to have some vaccinations that are absolutely critical for entry into Africa. One is rabies, and the second is yellow fever. You will need these certificates to cross borders in Africa and usually requested to have on paper presentation rather than from your app on your phone.
- You need to take into consideration the time of year you want to travel. Winter can be cool to cold especially if your trip is Safari, camping in tents, and a lot of walking.
- Cultural interaction with local people who have immense knowledge, love of country and a willingness to share it.
- Travel with a purpose as African safari supports worthy causes of conservation and the development of local communities, you

know that you have made your travel matter, leaves a feeling of win-win.

What to see in the Pretoria and Johannesburg area:

- There are a number of lion parks, some you can interact with the animals, especially the cubs.
- A trip to the diamond mine Cullinan and see where the largest diamond was found, and viewed regularly in London Tower on the royal crown and sceptre.
- A trip to the Voortrekker Monument which provided an extraordinary history related to the movement of the Voortrekkers who left the Cape area and established a colony in the 1830s south of Pretoria.
- We also had a look at the Place of Justice, where Nelson Mandela and his comrades were tried and sent to Robben Island for 18 years.
- There is so much history in Africa it is definitely worth a place on anybody's agenda.

You will be reminded from time to time by guides to make sure that you have everything secure such as money, passports, anything of value, will be just begging for someone to take them from you.

MARRIED TO A SUITCASE

Serengeti National Park and Plus Zanzibar Island

- There is absolutely no better way to get an authentic safari experience and really feel like you are part of the environment than camping in the Serengeti National Park in a tent for three nights and days.
- It was such a surreal experience to sit by the campfire, drinking a hot beverage and chatting with other like-minded adventurers in the middle of one of this world's most famous wildlife sanctuaries.
- It may not have all the luxuries you might be accustomed to back home, but nothing beats being out in the middle of the Serengeti and among the very wildlife you came to see.
- When we were on safari in the Serengeti, we got to see lions feasting on a wildebeest, which was a very surreal experience. It was sad to see a life lost, but we were happy to see that all of the little cubs' mouths would be fed that day.
- Serengeti National Park is one of the most amazing wildlife destinations in the world. Anyone on safari here will have a gallery full of just the most fabulous pictures. We were able to share each other's expert pictures to add to our stock.

Some important suggestions if you become a solo traveller and start linking countries together.

- Having a good travel agent who is well versed in your needs and has years of experience to share the beauty of your travel is a big plus and who has been there too.
- It is impossible to keep up with changes in all countries and their requirements. They can change from year to year. So always investigate what you require such as visas, vaccinations, documents crossing borders, etc.
- Make sure you have all the vaccinations, and the paperwork associated with them, on your App. is fine but always carry the paperwork. Inland border crossing can be demanding and often prefer the printed version to the app version – get an International Certificate of Vaccinations or Prophylaxis from a travel doctor and it's compact and easy to carry with my passport.
- Most passport centres also provide an ID card like your credit card which are

very useful and accepted in most areas not associated with official status such as; airports, border crossing and immigration.
- Have an emergency contact for back home. My agent is the first call who has an emergency list of my contacts. Make sure you keep all your lists up to date. Very easy to forget. Know your likes and dislikes and make them known to your agent who can alert organisers in advance.

CHAPTER EIGHT

Travelling Solo with Nursing in mind

When you mention being a nurse to people, they automatically will describe it as a person who gives direct care to us, will look after our loved ones when the time comes, images of selfless people such as the great Florence Nightingale, and lots of other examples that people will give you especially observing what you do.

The importance of nursing in the community

Nursing as a profession is so much more than some philosophy of spiritual meanings. A nurse today is someone with a very select set of skills, that can only be developed and honed by intense training, education, and discipline while being used in a prescribed ethical manner.

With such a combination of skills, ethics, and caring, nurses are the backbone of health care settings, tending to the individual needs of the patients and medical staff and the family of patients.

Nurse requirements in society:

- They have many skills and are often specialised in certain areas of healthcare, such as education, specialisation, computer skills and electronically controlled mechanisms, just to mention a few.
- They are employed in almost all professions, clergy, teaching, psychologists and philosophers providing a direction and moral compass in how to care for patients and each other.
- They are researchers and provide data to the public designed to improve health literacy

and promote health with physical and mental wellness.
- Nursing is global in nature and is facing global issues as well as country specific problems, like countries at war, emergencies caused by earthquakes, flooding, tsunamis, cyclones and the list goes on.
- Nursing puts people in the forefront of requiring staff in almost every profession that is dealing with the world and its people. In other words, there is no shortage of jobs available to nurses, aides and volunteers.
- Nursing became my mode of transport right from the very beginning when I completed my training in children's, general, and maternity certificates. I was ready for travel.
- Nursing on a cruise liner is a far cry from hospitals. Infections can travel faster; the tropics can create chest problems for people with heart conditions and chest infections.

Nursing positions are available in almost every aspect of community life and can often be useful when travelling from one destination to another either as a fully employed staff or a work-away nurse using one's skills as a monetary trade-off for passage to a different location.

Nursing in Australia

Nurses are always welcome in Australia, but the distance can be an obstacle for many who in the northern hemisphere can move between continents on shorter flights. Flights from Australia to Europe and America can involve long travel times and waiting in airports for connections.

Nursing today in Australia is not only interesting but very attractive in the variations now available for those in the nursing field as the education is more sophisticated

On a recent trip around the world, I spent some time in Bangkok as a volunteer in a refugee centre, I had the opportunity to care for mothers and babies for a short space of time. It was a pleasure to be able to answer their questions, to support them as they lived in a foreign country to their origin, and were adjusting to foreign expectations. I guess we had something in common. While not a refugee, I was very much an itinerant traveller far from my country of origin.

Global concerns that attract nurses' attention?

These concerns are worldwide but especially noticeable in Asian, African and South America but we don't have to go far from our own environment to see and witness poverty, sickness and homelessness. People sleeping on pavements, children homeless and unable to have a proper education.

Figure 1 Global concerns for nursing.

Benefits

By nursing overseas, you get to build skills, help diverse populations, work with colleagues who are equally dedicated to serving others, and build your professional portfolio.

Employers love it as it shows you as a global citizen. You are resourceful and have cross cultural skills. One of the biggest benefits, however, is the ability to gain perspective and realise that we have pretty amazing work prospects in the developed world.

Volunteer work in Asia and Africa to get involved in organisations that provide **Teaching** – Thailand, Vietnam, Myanmar, Fiji, Bali. **Health Care** – Bangkok, Legal and Law subjects for high School- Bali, Nepal, **Organic Farming** in the USA, are just some of the positions I have held as a volunteer and benefitted from in many ways.

- It's not all 3rd World Countries that are looking for volunteers, there are numerous advertisings for nurses and volunteers and especially for doctors, auxiliary staff to staff the outback in Australia, and many other countries in the pacific region.
- Explore and learn about yourself. And have a ready list of what you can offer and what you might want to get out of any situation.
- Watch advertisements for nursing placements overseas, you'll find how you can present yourself with what you have and what you would like to get from the situation. An interview is a two-way process not a one-way street.

Personal Benefits

- Expand your clinical knowledge and skill set.
- Sharpen your communication skills.
- Develop your confidence and resourcefulness.
- Build your personal and professional network.
- Become more attractive to employers.
- Have a great time learning.
- Mixing with people both workwise and educational.
- Some of the advantages of working in Australia as a nurse are: a hot climate and amazing beaches for a fulfilling life outside of work. A multi-cultural environment which makes it an exciting country to work in.
- Nursing in areas without a certificate provides experience and community involvement with cross cultures. You don't need to be qualified to do ESL (English Second Language) in most Asian countries and around the world. You will get support from the local teachers and WOW what an experience. I think I get more experience than the kids do. Sharpen your communication skills. Develop your confidence and resourcefulness. Build your personal and professional network. Become more attractive to employers.

Travel the world – nursing overseas

1. From volunteering in rural hospitals in South America to Asia as a student or nurse, to working for NGO/Humanitarian organisations in vulnerable communities, to working as a nurse in resorts or on super yachts on the high seas. This post has a great list across all areas of overseas nursing.
2. One of the benefits of nursing is the ability to travel the world and provide care in farfetched places. Being able to do this might be one of the most rewarding opportunities you can undertake.
3. Stay tuned as there are numerous posts popping up from humanitarian and aid nurses required sometimes at short notice as disasters occur without warning.
4. Overseas opportunities with a mix of volunteering, NGO/AID work, and some paid organisations. We haven't really focused on companies that help you get work, either part or full time overseas, i.e.: working in the USA or UAE through an agency, instead focusing on the more NGO/AID/Volunteering areas of nursing.
5. Some are aimed at students as part of their education and included in their selections of

subjects and others at qualified nurses who want to travel and explore the world.

The list is endless and gets expanded as the mix of careers and education have no boundaries. Be creative and take a chance, you will never be disappointed. I'm still active and mixing my degrees, personal experiences and adventures to enjoy what the world has to offer.

Other professionals can benefit from placements overseas which will enhance their experience

Volunteering is good for your resume because:
- It gives you valuable experience to add to your resume.
- It helps you expand your network.
- It can fill in gaps on your resume.
- It helps you learn and apply new skills.
- It increases your confidence.

Why is volunteer work on a resume beneficial?
1. Volunteer work can help you explore sectors where you have interests.
2. Voluntary work is also a great way to learn on the job and gain experience in an area where you may have minimal practice.

3. Volunteering can be an enriching experience for you and the organisation, as you both can benefit from your work.
4. Places where you can volunteer may include non-profit organisations, charities and local community businesses. In these environments, managers and team lead figures are likely to commend you for being enthusiastic and taking on unpaid responsibilities.

There are many reasons why you may consider showcasing your volunteer experience on your resume. Volunteer placements can set you apart from other candidates applying for paid positions or a place in an academic institution like a university.

Here are some examples of how detailing your volunteering experience can be helpful to your resume and job search:

- Showcase your transferable skills: These skills may apply to your future career and an industry you're passionate about.
- Explain breaks: Voluntary experience can fill gaps in employment and demonstrate initiative to develop in this time.
- Display your passion: Volunteering without pay shows you are passionate about an area.

- Demonstrate on-the-job experience: Students and recent graduates can show they have professional experience in their intended field by volunteering.
- Communicate your values: Voluntary work communicates your values, interests and work ethic to potential employers.
- Show development: Volunteer experience helps you demonstrate how you improved skills that align with the job's requirements.
- Read more: Everything You Need to Know about Volunteer Experience

What volunteer work looks good on a resume?

Volunteer work can add a lot of value to your resume. However, it is essential to know what type of volunteer work to add and exactly where to include it. You might use a resume to show employers that your skills and experience allow you to be an ideal candidate. It's advisable to focus on volunteer work that relates to the role you're applying for. Including relevant experience can showcase how you have used the skills detailed in a job description to help show that you are a good fit for the role:

Mentoring the children of vulnerable adults with disease prevention information and helpline services

Assisted people with disabilities, injuries and health conditions and helped them gain access to medication and support services.

CHAPTER NINE

How do I prepare to travel alone for the first time?

To prepare to travel alone for the first time, there are a few things that help to have a fun holiday.

- Do your research on what is required and any specialities associated with the areas you will visit.
- Chat with your travel agent to confirm travel details before your trip,
- Letting loved ones or friends who have Power of Attorney know your plan and where you'll be.

- Often a good idea to join up with groups for short tours in the beginning, The most important tip? Always trust your gut and be personally happy with your choices.
- You are doing what you want to experience and sharing when its useful to experience locations of interest. Get valuable information which helps you to be independent and informed.

Risks associated with Travelling solo

- When travelling alone, personal safety becomes more of an issue; stick to public lit areas at night.
- Language problems can lead to loneliness and not being able to share experiences.
- Eating alone can be a problem for some, listening to music with earphones can help.
- Illness or accidents can be a problem, make sure you are covered by insurance for medical assistance, hospitals, etc.
- Using a phone have their problems too, such as scam, being stolen, asking to have photos taken is risky.

- Pickpockets, assaults or robberies, losing passport or credit cards.
- Walking in high altitude places can lead to altitude sickness, be sure to take time to adjust to places before you commence walking.

The big advantage of course is you're going to do what you want to do, and you get assistance and lots of ideas from groups that you join which helps you in your own solo travel to.

Tips for travelling light during the day

It has its downside and yes, I have been robbed and in of all places, Peru, and I survived to live and tell the tale and I am still solo travelling. I learned a lot of lessons from this encounter about travelling light and who to contact.

You make it difficult to get access to your belongings.

1. Travel light, and any items that you have to carry during the day are concealed, a multi-pocketed jacket with inside pockets are difficult to pick pocket.

2. A small backpack to carry items like a bottle of water, snacks and sun lotion sachets for day trip.
3. Carry your passport only when going through some official area or of course going to the airport but you can carry a photocopy of your passport with all your particulars on it and on the back of it you can keep your emergency contact number. Laminate quite a few of these so that you can put them in various areas when travelling.
4. Other items your jacket can hide in the pockets i.e. Local cash, if necessary, when visiting markets, credit card, never carry more than one credit card, keep the rest at your hotel. Make sure you have a list of the credit card numbers in your diary, if you lose it, you can record the number to report its loss.
5. A disposable raincoat is small and easily carried in a pocket
6. I can carry my mobile phone, which can also be used as a camera, with a finger ring at the back to hold especially when taking photos.
7. String bags can act like backpacks, they come in small sizes, and can be useful when shopping and they are easy to roll up and put in jacket pocket.

There is only so much you can do and there is always the 5% that you can't anticipate and it might never happen to you. It just means that you need to take as many precautions as you can and learn from other people's demise.

Solo travel is one of the most rewarding experiences out there. Once you learn **how to travel solo**, the possibilities are endless. But in order to have the best experience possible, a little planning can go a long way. Whether you're a seasoned solo traveller or total newbie, check out the packing list in the Annex section of this book.

- Whether you're moving through airport security or just exploring a destination. Your multi-pocketed jacket will come in useful and leave your hands free. Cargo pants are a

similar idea with multiple pockets and can have the addition of being able to zip-off the legs and have shorts.
- Try noise cancelling headphones for travel, they make such a difference on noisy airplanes and trains. You can also change the audio settings to ambient noise so you can still hear your surroundings and be in-the-know. This is great for travelling solo. Make sure they fold up small.
- Look for items that are multi-purpose, mainly concentrated, biodegradable formula and can be used for laundry, dishes, and body wash. You can buy small size items at a supermarket on arrival. it's amazing how much use you get out of the bar of soap, like wiping down benches, cleaning the bathroom, and also many other items including laundry.
- There are several ways to keep your bag/case or backpack safe while travelling, as some nimble fingers are experts at removing items while you are preoccupied. Cases/bags can be locked with TSA locks, accepted with most check-ins at airports. Keys can get lost or difficult to find in airports. If you have carry-on items that have multi-pockets, like backpacks, try using self-locking nylon cables that are often used for holding up plants in

- the garden and carry a nail clipper to remove them when travelling.
- There are collapsible plastic bottles on the market used by campers which you can fill when you get passed the check-ins at the airport. These are often found in shops selling camping equipment. It's a good idea to carry some packs of hydration multiplier packs with electrolyte power to add to drinks for long air travel or hikes. When you're travelling solo, staying hydrated and feeling "with it" is important for not only your health but also your safety.
- Packing a first aid kit with items you need for small traumas. I also recommend adding some medicine like ibuprofen, Imodium, antihistamines, and bite cream - just in case. Carry some antibiotics that you know will agree with you. Your doctor can prescribe for you as it is often difficult getting early attention in foreign countries, and you can start your medication early. Ask your doctor for advice before you go.
- Safety is critical when travelling solo and your phone doubles as a safety tool. Whether you're using it for maps, transportation, contacting people, or something else, it's important that your phone is charged in case of an emergency. There are a number of small chargers on the

market today. Check that they hold multiple chargers and do the job quickly.
- If you are staying in hostels, you need to take care of security and providing personal items such as:
- If you plan on staying in hostels, I highly recommend packing your own microfiber towel. Many hostels have an extra cost for towels and laundry. By packing a **microfibre towel**, you can save money while still packing light. There are a few of them available on the market get one that is quick-drying and doesn't take up much space.
- An adapter is a must when travelling internationally. Use a multi-port charger, and it needs to be acceptable in Europe, Asia and the States. where you can charge up to six devices at once.
- Taking solo trips also means taking more safety precautions than you would if you were travelling with others. Since you can't travel with something like pepper spray, a **personal alarm** is the next best thing. And if you're staying anywhere alone (hotel, Airbnb, etc.), then I recommend packing a **personal door lock** for extra peace of mind. Easy to apply but difficult for the intruder to open, as they operate from inside rather than an external handle. Make sure

you leave this with objects you might present at the security section, as it is steel.
- It's always a good idea to pack flip-flops are also called thongs, and the name varies around the world. They're necessary for using in hostel showers, super handy in case you go swimming, and they double as slippers if need be. If they are fancy looking as mine are, then you can wear them as formal wear with sarongs or long dresses/pants.
- In your solo travel packing list, include some items you wouldn't mind leaving behind, like a t-shirt or some products. Op-shops are keen to get second hand clothes in good condition and will often exchange items on their racks for free.

Bring a diary to record details of holidays for later

As you may expect, travelling solo means you'll be doing some things alone. A travel journal makes a fantastic souvenir and, of course, filling in time when you're bored. I'm inclined to forget which year something happened. They tend to get moved together, and so the diaries are a great asset to locate where and what you did at certain times.

Laundry

Depending on where you stay and how you travel, you may need to wash clothes by hand. You may have access to laundry machines and services at your accommodation, or nearby, but the cost can add up, if you're on a long trip. Washing your clothes by hand can be more cost effective and sometimes more convenient and easily done in warm to hot countries.

Safety first

1. Keep important items like your passport and documents in one secure place when you travel. Mine are always inside my jacket and zipped. If you are not travelling then just leave them locked up at your accommodations during the day. Backpack or case. I always tie self-locking nylon cables on all my gear. It's a deterrent to nosy people who want to do a quick job. It slows the process of finding an item in a short space of time.
2. I also recommend copying all your important travel information (flight info, **travel insurance**, etc.) into one digital document or multi-folder if your travel takes in multiple destinations. In case of an emergency, you can

access all your information easily. I keep mine both digital and hard copy. A lot of airlines are asking for hard copy boarding passes, as small phones are difficult to scan.
3. Check-in with www.smarttraveller.gov.au which is a government service in Australia, that keeps you up to date with situations in the countries you intend to travel through on your trip. It's invaluable in our current climate of unrest in so many countries. They will also have a record of where you are and how best to retrieve you in case of danger.

A personal alarm or whistle is just another added layer of protection that will help to keep you safe while you're travelling by yourself. Use a personal alarm with a finger string I can keep when I'm walking around towns or buildings. I can pull the string and the alarm is piercing. Many muggers and attackers are actually quite cowardly and will only attack you if they think they're going to get away with it. A loud noise coming from a whistle or alarm scares people like them off.

Carrying pepper spray is actually prohibited in many countries and cannot be taken through the airport. Plus, pepper spray can be wrestled away from you and used against you.

Cash and Cards

Do your homework and investigate with locals or your travel agent, if you need any cash going through the airport or crossing borders (very common in Africa, Americas, South America,) so you only have the cash you need and a credit card may be sufficient. There are tons of opinions on best money practices while travelling abroad. As a general rule, it's a good idea to keep some cash on hand. If you can't get local currency before travelling, bring cash in USD so you can at least do a cash exchange in your new destination, usually at the airport. Tap-on is very common in most countries in Asia unless remote, like monasteries, rural areas and hiking.

Packing List check the list in the annex area to complete your own list for your trip.

CHAPTER TEN

Travelling within countries in conflict

www.smarttraveller.gov.au major area for the following information.

Treat conflict in countries Serious

When countries are classified as dangerous versus safe doesn't save you when you travel. You can be just as vulnerable in a safe zone as you would be in a danger zone. I have found myself in tricky situations and possibly felt uncomfortable, but like all things I've lived to tell the tale.

Before you go, do some research on all the areas that you are likely to visit, especially as a solo traveller. You may have to cross many borders and encounter different people on your travel. There are a number of countries that have services available to recognise the conditions of the countries that you are going to visit. In Australia we have a service called www.smarttraveller.gov.au which anyone can sign into prior to travelling and let them know which countries you are about to visit. Each day they will send you an update on areas which are classified as high danger versus average to none. The service cannot help you to get out of the problem you're in and sometimes there are no consulates in the area so check what you can avail if in danger.

Remember, it's not just the countries you are visiting also the countries you may transit through on your travels in which circumstances might also change. Smart Traveler has consular partners such as Canada, the United Kingdom, and the United States, and reports on Asian countries if there are likely to be problems. Items you often see, things like major protests or unrest in particular cities, new entries if there has been a natural disaster in the area, or sometimes they referred to areas to take reasonable care, and may give you some reasons why. I find it very useful as I do frequent solo travels which take in more than one country and often cross more than one border in order to get from one to the other.

Travel insurance

Before booking travel, make sure to purchase your travel insurances and ensure you are aware of the situation in any of the areas you are likely to travel in. If there is a likelihood of a disturbance or danger, the insurance that you have may not cover you if it's not specifically mentioned in the insurance policy.

It's also worthwhile to read your policy before you sign:

1. **Does the policy cover cancellations or change of conditions?**
2. **Does it cover Covid related issues?**
3. **What about retrieval from a danger zone? Will you be rescued early or get access to a flight to leave the country?**
4. **Ask for clarity on any of the clauses you're not sure of as it may be important for your purpose.**

No matter how safe the country may be advertised as okay, you still need to use common sense and to look out for suspicious behaviour just as you probably would do anywhere, even at home.

Danger is usually classified in various levels from 1 to 4 in most cases.

Level I is no risk area does not mean that problems can't occur or that you are protected in some miraculous way. Every day we read on newspapers and TV of unprovoked attacks in our own city or around the world. Always monitor the media and look for sources of changes in travelling conditions, health situations and security concerns. Look for variations in your surroundings from day-to-day, some things might just look out of place, different.

Level II risk area is often identified in a city as not a safe area to be exploring, especially if you're a solo traveller. I find when I am working as a volunteer teaching in Asia, I will be advised that certain areas of cities that I am in may not be ideally suitable for casual travelling and exploring. The locals may offer to accompany you when shopping.

This is usually associated with:

- A weak law enforcement.
- Lack of public services such as police force or may not respond quickly in the situation.
- There may have been past histories of political unrest or short-term increases in domestic violence or terrorism.

It's also good to discuss with the locals on your arrival as to what transport is safe for you to travel in, what taxies to take, what to wear and what not to wear, and be aware of what behaviour may offend or break the law.

Level III is serious and potentially life-threatening risks. This can make your destination unsafe for tourism and unsuitable for travellers.

- Usually, the news broadcasts such things as terrorism, kidnapping, travel interruptions, violent crime, civil unrest, or of course none of the above,
- There could be widespread infectious diseases which can have a catastrophic effect.
- There are other major incidents which can occur that will cause inconvenience such as natural disasters, global pandemics which

could be a risk to most travellers as you may not be immune to a new strain.

- *Level IV, is a category which could cover any of the above three but generally it is described as the unexpected. A sudden death at home, accidents, hospitalisation, anything that is likely to create a sudden disruption in your plans.*

If you need to go to these areas as part of your work, or personal need, always check that your insurance will cover you in these situations. Most governments are very limited in how and when they can help you if you get into trouble. Conditions could change at any time, so you need to be prepared for maybe an extended stay or significant disruptions in your travel.

Level IV Do not travel unless you really have to.

TRAVELLING WITHIN COUNTRIES IN CONFLICT

If you're in this situation you should consider leaving immediately if that's possible and safe to do so. If you do travel get professional security advice regarding the area you are in. Your travel insurance may not cover you in the current situation and consulates may not be in position to help you.

Almost every condition will be unsafe and extreme in this situation it may be due to terrorist attack, conflict between two countries where borders are concerned, widespread infection and highly contagious diseases, it may be a combination of a number of risks and unstable situations for example the Israeli/ Palestinian conflict of 2024. If you travel in these situations, you are at high risk of death, imprisonment, kidnapping, or serious injury if attacked.

You may well find that consulates are unable to provide up-to-date minute to minute assistance due to the lack of communication. Even the consulates cannot protect their advisors and officials or ambassadors and approval for travel would have to be given by the highest authority and making rigorous risk assessments. If you leave the area at your own risk then it is wise to at least inform people where you are and what you've done, as they may well not be able to provide rescue services for you.

Checklist before you go

Always check **your travel insurance polic**y and consider the items on your travel list are covered or not covered by a normal insurance, you may have to improvise and check with other policies that may cover what you require. Insurances may become more expensive as you add more cover, such as age, physical and mental disorders, anything outside their nominated items.

Governments usually research the political and security situations from a variety of sources not just one which might be misrepresenting the severity of the situation. You need to understand the risks and regularly check the news and social media to keep up-to-date and informed.

It is **essential to understand the health situation and risks for entry to your destination** may require specific vaccinations, specific insurance coverage, local restrictions may not be affecting the whole country, pandemic restrictions may apply to group travel which might be in risk of transmission.

Pre-book your accommodation in advance in safe areas with appropriate security. Get advice from your travel agent and from local travel agents as to what areas are safe and what areas to avoid.

Minimise your time spent in airports by scheduling direct flights if possible or short stay between flights to avoid stopovers in high-risk airports. Stay as short a time as possible if the area sounds risky to you and eliminate unnecessary activities.

While most hotels have a certain **element of security such as locking doors** and having contingency plans for emergency evacuation. Hostels and lodgings may not have as sophisticated measures. Carry a separate locking device for the door which is very easy to use but prevents people on the other side being able to open the door while you're asleep. **Make sure it is the first thing you unlock on your site especially if there is a fire or a danger in which you may need to make an emergency evacuation.**

This is one area that very few people consult before they go on a trip especially if the trip is going to be longer than usual, taking in a few months.

Leave an up-to-date arrangement with enduring power of attorney in case you may be incapacitated or worse die, so those back at home will be able to proceed without your presence. Also designate in your insurance that you want to have retrieval or cremation in the case of death, so that you will be sent back to your own country as part of that insurance.

While you are travelling checklist

With the amount of Wi-Fi equipment that we have available to us in today's travelling it is easy for us to stay up-to-date with activities in the area you are travelling and possibly in the area that you are going to travel in.

Beware of health risks in your area, danger of terrorist attacks, local news. Be prepared to change your plans and stay in touch with your travel agent who may be aware of situations that are not being broadcast in your area.

Stay alert and beware of activity in your environment such as suspicious activity or items and report anything of concern to local authorities, and to your travel agent who may not be in this country and may not be aware of disturbances.

You may be excited about your own travel, but don't discuss your travel plans with strangers. Never share personal information such as phone numbers or addresses, especially in the local area, with people asking questions without good reason.

Don't discuss your plans for risk management strategies that might be overheard by very long ears in your vicinity. People using social media to share information about their travel arrangements. Never a good idea because you have so many people who have access to that information without your knowledge.

Avoid travelling alone, especially after dark, in areas not considered safe in the city or your environment, especially on long trips.

You never know who is watching you.

1. Don't stand out in a crowd, dress down in casual gear or as near enough as the locals.
2. Delete the handbags, and accessories like expensive jewellery.
3. Don't carry your passport unless you must.
4. Carry a copy of your emergency number on the back of your picture and laminate it.

Using taxis as a single person on my solo travels

1. Always check out the taxi agent. If I'm doing a volunteer job, I ask the manager to order a taxi for me, as they often have a partnership with particular taxi drivers.

2. Monastery or similar organisations will have specific taxi groups to and from the area.
3. If you are driving in strange areas, always keep your windows closed, lock your door when leaving, check that there is no change in your vehicle on your return, that you have enough fuel to get you from A to B and return if necessary.

- As a solo person travelling taking public transport especially after dark can be unsafe you may have to watch out for people who are watching you if you're aware of it, or you have somebody to meet you at your destination is a good idea.
- Never take anything that is offered to you in the course of your travel, especially taking it across borders or through airports. If it contains drugs or illegal substances, you may well find yourself in jail, arrested at the site and your consulate may have little or no control over the situation.
- Not a good idea to entertain strangers in your hotel room or accepting invitations to unknown or remote places that they may have selected to meet, not even with a friend. We read too much about the consequences of such meetings and it cannot be undone once it occurs.

- It's a good idea to maintain good hygiene and physical distance in most situations where crowds are, especially when interacting with other people.
- Always have a plan for emergency evacuation when the environment becomes unsafe as you may have to do this at short notice.
- Always carry a charger for your phone and make sure your own phone is fully charged before you leave the house. Have urgent numbers to contacts, up-to-date and ready for use, let people know where you are going especially if you are doing volunteer work, visiting particular people, involved in some activity that the rest of the group is not involved in, the list is endless here just let people know where you are and who you may be with, it may well save your life.
- Always maintain contingency kits such as medical supplies, medication that is specifically yours, sufficient food and water for treks, and emergency provisions with you that might be necessary in an emergency such as when camping.

What can consulates do.

Most consulates may be able to:

- Issue a replacement passport or travel documents for a fee (had this in Peru), provide details for local doctors and hospitals if required, can provide advice and support if you are the victim of a serious assault, provide contacts for you in the case of welfare or arrested or detained they can provide advice and support in the case of death of relatives overseas, missing persons, and kidnappings.
- Consulates can contact family or friends with your agreement, voting services, can witness particular documents and make arrangements for you in the case of international terrorism, civil disturbances or natural disasters.

What consulates can't do on your behalf

1. They can't guarantee safety and security in another country or make travel arrangements on your behalf, or provide legal advice or interpreters to translate documents, nor intervene in another country's court procedures, legal matters or commercial disputes.

2. Cannot investigate crimes or debts overseas, carry out searches for missing people, this is the responsibility of the local authorities.
3. Consulates cannot get you better conditions in prison or prevent you from being deported, or paying a fine, reinforcing custodian agreement overseas or compelling a country to decide a custodial case.
4. Consulates cannot arrange visas, licenses to work, or residential permits for other countries, intervene in immigration customs of quarantine matters in other countries.
5. They are not areas for you to store luggage or personal items, receive personal postal items on your behalf.

What to do if you are mugged or attacked

1. Find your way to the nearest police station and have your attack registered.
2. Have police report stamped and available for border crossing
3. You will need a police report if you lose your passport.
4. You will require a police report to claim insurance refund when you return home.
5. If you need medical attention, make sure your insurance is adequately covering what is required.
6. Make your way to the nearest consulate of your country's origin as you may be able to get an emergency passport. It is costly when you lose a passport.
7. If you get an emergency passport you may have to go to the immigration department to have an exit slip inserted into your passport in order to leave the country.

Annexes

Checklists for easy access in the case of emergencies

Complete Travel Packing Checklist

Destination _____ No. Days _____
Weather _____

Essentials	**Toiletries**	**Clothing**
Passport/ID card/copies	Toothbrush/toothpaste	Casual tops
Visa /boarding pass	Body wash/soap	Dress tops
Confirmation receipts	Face wash	T-shirts

Essentials	Toiletries	Clothing
Travel arrangements	Deodorant	jeans will/ casual pounds
Emergency documents	Eyedrops/ contact solution	Jackets
Emergency contacts	Shampoo/ conditioner	Shorts/dresses
Credit cards/ cash	Hand/body lotion	Blazer/suit/ coats
Copies of passport and documents		Sweaters/ cardigans
	Health / beauty	Sports ware/ casual
Funds/cash		Swimwear/ cover-ups
Wallet/pen	Basic medications not prescriptions	Pyjamas/ nighties
Credit cards	Basic first aid items	Socks /bras/ hosiery
Cash	Vitamins	
Insurance cards	Sunscreen/lip balm	
Itinerary	Shaving items	**Shoes**

ANNEXES

Essentials	Toiletries	Clothing
Other items	Hair products/shampoo	
Mobile phone and charger	Hair tools/dryers/straightener	Dress shoes/heels
Keys	Brush/hair ties/bobby pins	Joggers/boots
Glasses/contact lens	Make up/perfume	Sandals/sports shoes
Rx medications	Feminine care items	Specialities footwear for hiking/athletic shoes
Binoculars	Tweezers/Q-tips/tissues	
	Cotton buds/nail polish	**Miscellaneous items**
Personal Comforts		
	Accessories	Address book/guidebook
Neck pillow		Maps/directions
Jacket light/heavy	Sunglasses	All charges Adapters / converters

MARRIED TO A SUITCASE

Essentials	Toiletries	Clothing
Socks light/thick	Watch/jewellery	
Eye mask	Belts/scarfs/hat	
Headphone / Ear plugs	Purses/umbrella	
Water bottle/snacks		
Change of clothing	**Electronics**	
Hand sanitiser	iPad /tablet E-reader	
	Laptop	
	Camera	

http//www.smartraveller.gov.au/while-youre-away/crime/robbed-mugged#safety

What to do after a robbery, mugging or theft in a foreign country

Keep Calm

Immediately

Your safety is your first priority. You can replace your property, but you can't be replaced.

Get to safety. If you're already safe, stay put. If not, find somewhere well populated and well lit. If possible, find a police station, hospital or major hotel with security guards.

Don't chase after the perpetrator or try to track them down yourself. They may respond with violence. Let local police handle it.

Health

Look after your health. If you're injured, get medical assistance.

We publish local emergency contacts in the travel advice for each destination.

We also keep lists of local hospitals in each destination with doctors who speak English. Contact your nearest embassy or consulate, or call your 24-hour Consular Emergency Centre nearest to your location. Or the Federal Police immediately if you are Australian.

Report to the police

Report the crime to the local police. We publish local emergency numbers in the travel advice for each destination.

Be aware that a local crime is a matter for local authorities. The Governments are limited in how and when it can get involved.

Should I report the attack to the Police?

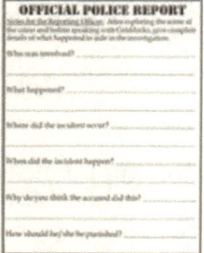

It's up to you if you'll report the robbery, theft, mugging or carjacking.

However, be aware that failing to report a crime is illegal in some countries. If so, and local police find out about it, they may arrest you. Before deciding not to report it, check the local law.

If you're the victim of a carjacking, failing to report the crime comes with other risks.

If the thief uses the car to break other laws (e.g. speeding), the police may think you were driving. They could arrest you for someone else's crime. Without a police report, you can't claim on car or travel insurance.

Gather evidence
You'll need to provide the police with everything you can remember about the incident. As soon as you can, write down the details.

Consider the perpetrator's physical attributes. This can include assumptions on age, weight, gender and nationality. Also remember their skin, hair and eye colour.

Remember what they said. Also, how they said it. Details that may seem small on the surface can help the police in their investigation.

Think about what you were doing at the time. Also think about what else was happening around you.

What you were doing, and where, can also impact your travel insurance claim.

Try to remember who else was nearby when it happened. Criminals often work in groups. For example, a person you interacted with may have been the decoy for a pickpocket or bag snatch.

Be careful about accusing someone of theft. Don't just assume it's the hotel staff or another guest. If you make an accusation without proof, local police could arrest you for defamation.

Get a police report

Your insurer may also ask for some of these details and a copy of the police report.

Prevent fraud and identity theft

If someone has taken your passport, phone or bank card, you're at risk of fraud or identity theft (Australian Federal Police). You must act quickly, as the passport is the property of the Government from whom you purchased it from, if you have Dual Citizenship or your country of origin if not.

ANNEXES

Stolen passport
If someone has stolen your passport:

Contact your nearest Australian embassy or consulate, or call the 24-hour Consular Emergency Centre in Australia on +61 2 6261 3305.

In some countries, you could also be arrested or jailed for not having your passport on you. Without it, you won't be able to leave the country to get home.

See from your own country about loss of passports.

Stolen phone
If someone has stolen your phone, use the remote wipe feature promptly.

Otherwise, if someone finds your phone and gets past your lock screen, they could access your personal information. This includes saved passwords and banking log-in details.

Learn more about how to remotely wipe your mobile phone. See what to do if your iPhone or iPad is lost or stolen (Apple) or how to find, lock or erase and Android device (Google).

Stolen credit or debit card
If someone has stolen your debit or credit card, contact your bank to cancel it immediately.

Criminals can use your cards to quickly empty your accounts, and run up a debt to the maximum limit. Most Australian financial institutions have 24-hour emergency numbers you can call from overseas.

Contact your insurer
Travel insurer

Contact your travel insurer. Tell them what happened.

You may wish to make a claim to:
replace your stolen property

repair or replace any damaged items from the incident

cancel or change your travel plans

Get medical assistance if you're injured.

Exempt the car hire insurance excess, if you've been carjacked.

Check the fine print on your policy. Confirm what you can claim. Find out how to claim.

You can also find contact details of travel insurers in Australia on Find an Insurer (Insurance Council of Australia).

Car insurer, if carjacked

Carjacking is a violent, road-based crime. It's also a form of robbery.

The car insurance claims process is separate to your travel insurance claim. Most travel insurance policies don't include car insurance. However, some include car hire excess cover.

Car insurance is usually through the hire company. There may be a very large excess.

Ask the hire company about their car insurance claims process, and their excess.

Replace your stolen items

If you need a replacement passport, we can help. See our page on passports.

If you need cash urgently, contact your travel insurer, family or friends. The Australian Government can't give you money.

If you need new credit or debit cards, contact your bank. Most have processes to express post replacement cards to your hotel or a local post office while travelling overseas.

To replace other stolen items you need while overseas, try to find local vendors. Understand that some items readily available in Australia may be hard to get overseas. This includes medications.

About The Author

Olivia is a person who seeks adventure, finds strength in being involved in a variety of cultures, and discovers her true self in every destination. Olivia has been an independent person from a very early age and likes mixing with different cultures, shares her talents with a variety of people as a volunteer in a number of capacities ranging from Teaching English as second language, working in organic farms, work-away passage on migrant ships from UK to Australia and beyond, just to mention a few. Olivia enjoys travelling alone. It increases her independence, increases her confidence to chart her own paths in life and find beauty in her own thoughts and expectations. There is adventure in every solo travel where one gets to become the storyteller of many exciting and extraordinary tales.

www.ingramcontent.com/pod-product-compliance
Lightning Source LLC
Chambersburg PA
CBHW030303100526
44590CB00012B/506